YUMMY ADVENTURES
Cooking with Kids cookbook

Easy and Delicious Recipes for Kids to Make

James Stott

We really hope that you enjoy this culinary adventure and would ask that if you are enjoying the recipes here that you consider placing a review or star rating on Amazon using the link or QR code below. Your review really helps others to find this book and it would be really appreciated.

ReviewYummyAdventures

INTRODUCTION

Welcome to Yummy Adventures: Cooking with Kids, a delightful cookbook filled with easy and delicious recipes designed especially for young chefs! This book is more than just a collection of recipes; it's an invitation to embark on a culinary journey with your children, exploring the joys of cooking together.

Cooking is an essential life skill, and introducing kids to the kitchen at an early age can foster a lifelong love for good food and healthy eating. This cookbook aims to make cooking fun and accessible for kids, encouraging creativity and confidence as they learn to prepare a variety of tasty meals and snacks.

Each recipe in this book is crafted to be simple and engaging, with step-by-step instructions that are easy for kids to follow. From breakfast treats to delightful desserts, every dish is designed to be both nutritious and appealing to young taste buds. We've included colorful photos and helpful tips to make the cooking process even more enjoyable.

Yummy Adventures: Cooking with Kids is perfect for family time in the kitchen, whether you're looking to teach your kids basic cooking skills or simply want to create memorable moments together. As you flip through these pages, you'll find recipes that cater to a range of skill levels and dietary preferences, ensuring that every child can find something they love to make and eat.

Let this cookbook be your guide as you discover the magic of cooking with kids. Get ready to create delicious memories and embark on a fun-filled culinary adventure with your little ones. Happy cooking!

Contents

BREAKFAST

FRUIT AND YOGURT PARFAIT

Prep Time: 10 mins   **Cook Time: 00 mins**   **Serving: 2 parfaits**

INGREDIENTS

- 1 cup Greek yogurt
- 1 cup granola
- 1/2 cup mixed berries
- 1 banana, sliced
- 2 tablespoons honey (optional)

INSTRUCTIONS

1. In two glasses, layer 1/4 cup of Greek yogurt at the bottom of each glass.
2. Place 1/4 cup granola layer on top of the yogurt. Then, add a layer of mixed berries and banana slices.
3. Repeat the layering process with another 1/4 cup Greek yogurt, followed by 1/4 cup granola and the leftover mixed fruits and banana slices.
4. Drizzle one tablespoon honey over each parfait, if desired. Serve immediately.

Nutritional Values (per serving):

Calories: 250, Protein: 12g, Fat: 8g,
Carbohydrates: 36g, Fiber: 5g, Sugar: 18g

HOMEMADE PANCAKES

Prep Time: 10 mins   **Cook Time: 15 mins**   **Serving: 4**

INGREDIENTS

- 1 cup all-purpose flour
- 2 tablespoons sugar
- 1 tablespoon baking powder
- 1/2 teaspoon salt
- 1 cup milk
- 1 large egg
- 2 tablespoons melted butter
- 1 teaspoon vanilla extract
- Maple syrup and fresh fruit for serving

INSTRUCTIONS

1. Take the large shallow bowl and toss the flour, sugar, baking powder, and salt. In another bowl, toss the milk, egg melted butter, and vanilla extract.
2. Ladle liquid ingredients into the dry ingredients and mix until just combined.
3. Put the non-stick skillet or griddle over moderate heat and lightly grease with butter/oil.
4. Drop 1/4 cup batter for every pancake. Cook until bubbles form on the upper surface and the edges look set, then flip and cook until golden brown.
5. Serve warm with sweetener syrup and fresh fruit.

Nutritional Values (per serving):

Calories: 210, Protein: 6g, Fat: 8g,
Carbohydrates: 28g, Fiber: 1g, Sugar: 8g

MINI BREAKFAST PIZZAS

| Prep Time: 10 mins | Cook Time: 10 mins | Serving: 4 |

INGREDIENTS

- 4 whole wheat English muffins, split
- 1/2 cup tomato sauce
- 1 cup shredded mozzarella cheese
- 1/2 cup sliced bell peppers
- 8 Pepperoni slices
- 1/2 cup sliced cherry tomatoes
- 1/4 teaspoon dried oregano

INSTRUCTIONS

1. Preheat oven to 375°F (190°C). Put the halved English muffins on a baking sheet.
2. Spread a tablespoon tomato sauce on every muffin half. Sprinkle with shredded mozzarella cheese.
3. Top with sliced bell peppers, pepperoni, and cherry tomatoes. Sprinkle with dried oregano.
4. Bake for 8-10 minutes until cheese melts thoroughly and bubbly. Serve warm.

Nutritional Values (per serving):

Calories: 200, Protein: 10g, Fat: 8g,
Carbohydrates: 24g, Fiber: 4g, Sugar: 4g

BANANA OATMEAL MUFFINS

Prep Time: 10 mins   **Cook Time: 20 mins**   **Serving: 12 muffins**

INGREDIENTS

- 2 ripe bananas, mashed
- 1 cup rolled oats
- 1 cup all-purpose flour
- 1/2 cup brown sugar
- 1/2 cup milk
- 1 large egg
- 1/4 cup melted butter
- 1 teaspoon baking powder
- 1/2 teaspoon baking soda
- 1/4 teaspoon salt
- 1/2 cup chocolate chips

INSTRUCTIONS

1. Preheat oven to 350°F (175°C). Arrange the muffin tin with paper liners or grease with cooking spray.
2. Take the large shallow bowl and toss the mashed bananas, oats, flour, brown sugar, milk, egg, and melted butter until well combined.
3. Add baking powder, soda, and salt, and mix until just combined.
4. Fold in the chocolate chips. Divide the batter among the muffin cups equally.
5. Bake for 17-20 minutes until toothpick inserted and comes out clean.
6. Cool the muffins, then transfer to the serving plate.

Nutritional Values (per serving):

Calories: 180, Protein: 4g, Fat: 7g,
Carbohydrates: 28g, Fiber: 2g, Sugar: 14g

16

VEGGIE OMELET

Prep Time: 10 mins   **Cook Time: 10 mins**   **Serving: 2**

INGREDIENTS

- 4 large eggs
- 1/4 cup milk
- 1/4 teaspoon salt
- 1/4 teaspoon black pepper
- 1/2 cup chopped bell peppers
- 1/2 cup chopped spinach
- 1/4 cup chopped tomatoes
- 1/4 cup shredded cheese
- 1 tablespoon olive oil

INSTRUCTIONS

1. In a deep-bottom bowl, toss the eggs, milk, salt, and black pepper.
2. Heat one tbsp oil in a non-stick skillet over medium heat.
3. Ladle egg mixture and cook for 1-2 minutes, until it begins to set.
4. Add the chopped bell peppers, spinach, tomatoes, and shredded cheese to one-half of the omelet.
5. Fold the other half over the filling and cook for another 2-3 minutes until the eggs are fully set. Serve warm.

Nutritional Values (per serving):

Calories: 220, Protein: 14g, Fat: 15g,
Carbohydrates: 6g, Fiber: 2g, Sugar: 3g

BREAKFAST QUESADILLAS

Prep Time: 10 mins   **Cook Time: 10 mins**   **Serving: 4**

INGREDIENTS

- 4 whole wheat tortillas
- 4 large eggs, scrambled
- 1 cup shredded cheese
- 1/2 cup diced bell peppers
- 1/2 cup diced tomatoes
- 1 tablespoon butter

INSTRUCTIONS

1. Put the non-stick skillet over medium heat and melt the butter.
2. Place a tortilla in the skillet and sprinkle half of the shredded cheese on one half of the tortilla.
3. Add scrambled eggs, diced bell peppers, and diced tomatoes on top of the cheese.
4. Sprinkle the leftover cheese over the vegetables and eggs, and fold the tortilla in half.
5. Cook for 2-3 minutes on every side until the tortilla is crispy.
6. Repeat with the leftover tortillas. Cut into wedges and serve warm.

Nutritional Values (per serving):

Calories: 300, Protein: 15g, Fat: 17g,
Carbohydrates: 22g, Fiber: 4g, Sugar: 3g

OVERNIGHT OATS

Prep Time: 5 mins   **Cook Time: 00 mins**   **Serving: 2**

INGREDIENTS

- 1 cup rolled oats
- 1 cup milk (any type)
- 1/2 cup Greek yogurt
- 2 tablespoons honey
- 1/2 teaspoon vanilla extract
- 1/2 cup mixed fruit (for topping)

INSTRUCTIONS

1. In a jar or container, toss the rolled oats, milk, Greek yogurt, honey, and vanilla extract. Stir well to combine.
2. Seal the container and refrigerate overnight.
3. Next morning, give the oats a good stir and top with mixed fruit. Serve chilled.

Nutritional Values (per serving):

Calories: 250, Protein: 10g, Fat: 6g,
Carbohydrates: 40g, Fiber: 5g, Sugar: 18g

SMOOTHIE BOWLS

Prep Time: 10 mins   **Cook Time: 00 mins**   **Serving: 2**

INGREDIENTS

- 2 cups frozen mixed fruit (e.g., berries, banana, mango)
- 1 cup Greek yogurt or milk (any type)
- 1 tablespoon honey (optional)
- 1/2 cup granola
- 1/4 cup nuts
- 1/2 cup fresh fruit (for topping)

INSTRUCTIONS

1. In a blender, combine the frozen mixed fruit, Greek yogurt or milk, and honey. Blend until smooth and thick.
2. Pour the smoothie mixture into bowls. Top with granola, nuts, and fresh fruit. Serve immediately.

Nutritional Values (per serving):

Calories: 300, Protein: 12g, Fat: 10g,
Carbohydrates: 45g, Fiber: 6g, Sugar: 25g

BREAKFAST BURRITOS

Prep Time: 10 mins   **Cook Time: 10 mins**   **Serving: 4**

INGREDIENTS

- 4 large tortillas
- 6 large eggs, scrambled
- 1 cup shredded cheese
- 1/2 cup cooked sausage or bacon, crumbled
- 1/2 cup diced bell peppers
- 1/4 cup diced onions
- 1 tablespoon butter

INSTRUCTIONS

1. Put the non-stick skillet and melt the butter over medium heat.
2. Add diced bell peppers and onions, and cook until softened. Add scrambled eggs and cook until fully set.
3. Place a tortilla on a flat surface and add a portion of scrambled eggs, crumbled sausage or bacon, and shredded cheese.
4. Roll up the tortilla, folding in the sides to enclose the filling. Repeat with the leftover tortillas. Serve warm.

Nutritional Values (per serving):

Calories: 350, Protein: 18g, Fat: 20g, Carbohydrates: 25g, Fiber: 3g, Sugar: 3g

PEANUT BUTTER BANANA TOAST

Prep Time: 5 mins **Cook Time: 00 mins** **Serving: 2**

INGREDIENTS

- 2 slices whole grain bread, toasted
- 2 tablespoons peanut butter
- 1 banana, sliced
- 2 teaspoons honey (optional)

INSTRUCTIONS

1. Spread 1 tablespoon of peanut butter on every slice of toasted whole grain bread.
2. Top each slice with banana slices. Drizzle 1 teaspoon of honey over each toast, if desired. Serve immediately.

Nutritional Values (per serving):

Calories: 250, Protein: 7g, Fat: 11g,
Carbohydrates: 32g, Fiber: 4g, Sugar: 14g

LUNCH

INGREDIENTS

- 8 slices of bread (whole grain, white, or your choice)
- 1/2 pound deli meats (turkey, ham, chicken, etc.)
- 8 slices of cheese (cheddar, Swiss, American, etc.)
- Lettuce leaves
- Tomato slices
- Cucumber slices
- Mustard, mayonnaise, and other condiments

BUILD-YOUR-OWN SANDWICHES

Prep Time: 10 mins   **Cook Time: 00 mins**   **Serving: 4**

INSTRUCTIONS

1. Set out all the ingredients on a table or counter.
2. Let kids choose their preferred bread, deli meats, cheese, and vegetables.
3. Allow them to spread condiments on the bread slices and assemble their sandwiches. Serve immediately.

Nutritional Values (per serving):

Calories: 300, Protein: 18g, Fat: 12g, Carbohydrates: 30g, Fiber: 4g, Sugar: 4g

VEGGIE WRAPS

Prep Time: 10 mins **Cook Time: 00 mins** **Serving: 4**

INGREDIENTS

- 4 whole wheat wraps
- 1 cup hummus
- 1 cup shredded carrots
- 1 cup cucumber slices
- 1 cup lettuce leaves

INSTRUCTIONS

1. Lay out the whole wheat wraps on a flat surface. Spread 1/4 cup of hummus on every wrap.
2. Evenly distribute the shredded carrots, cucumber slices, and lettuce leaves on top of the hummus.
3. Roll up the wraps tightly and cut them in half. Serve immediately.

Nutritional Values (per serving):

Calories: 250, Protein: 8g, Fat: 10g, Carbohydrates: 32g, Fiber: 8g, Sugar: 3g

TURKEY AND CHEESE ROLL-UPS

Prep Time: 10 mins   **Cook Time: 00 mins**   **Serving: 4**

INSTRUCTIONS

1. Lay out the turkey slices on a flat surface. Spread 1/2 tbsp cream cheese on every turkey slice.
2. Place a slice of cheese on top of each turkey slice. Roll up the turkey slices tightly. Serve with crackers.

INGREDIENTS

- 8 slices of turkey
- 4 slices of cheese (cheddar, Swiss, American, etc.)
- 4 tablespoons cream cheese
- Crackers (for serving)

Nutritional Values (per serving):

Calories: 200, Protein: 12g, Fat: 14g, Carbohydrates: 6g, Fiber: 1g, Sugar: 2g

INGREDIENTS

- 4 mini pitas
- 1/2 cup tomato sauce
- 1 cup shredded mozzarella cheese
- Favorite pizza toppings (pepperoni, bell peppers, mushrooms, etc.)

MINI PITA PIZZAS

Prep Time: 10 mins   **Cook Time: 10 mins**   **Serving: 4**

INSTRUCTIONS

1. Preheat oven to 375°F (190°C). Place the mini pitas on a baking sheet.

2. Spread 2 tablespoons of tomato sauce on every pita. Sprinkle shredded mozzarella cheese on the sauce's top surface.

3. Let kids add their favorite pizza toppings. Bake for 8-10 minutes until the cheese melts and bubbly. Serve warm.

Nutritional Values (per serving):

Calories: 220, Protein: 10g, Fat: 8g, Carbohydrates: 28g, Fiber: 2g, Sugar: 4g

ANTIPASTO SKEWERS

Prep Time: 10 mins **Cook Time: 00 mins** **Serving: 4**

INGREDIENTS

- 16 cherry tomatoes
- 16 cheese cubes (cheddar, mozzarella, or your choice)
- 16 olives (green or black)
- 8 slices of salami, folded
- 8 wooden skewers

INSTRUCTIONS

1. Thread 2 cherry tomatoes, 2 cheese cubes, 2 olives, and 1 folded slice of salami onto each skewer.
2. Repeat with the leftover skewers. Serve immediately.

Nutritional Values (per serving):

Calories: 180, Protein: 10g, Fat: 14g, Carbohydrates: 4g, Fiber: 1g, Sugar: 2g

TUNA SALAD STUFFED AVOCADO

| Prep Time: 10 mins | Cook Time: 00 mins | Serving: 2 |

INSTRUCTIONS

1. In a deep-bottom bowl, toss the tuna, Greek yogurt, diced celery, diced bell pepper, and lemon juice.
2. Powder it with salt and crushed pepper to taste.
3. Spoon the tuna salad into the halved avocados. Serve immediately.

INGREDIENTS

- 1 can tuna, drained
- 1/4 cup Greek yogurt
- 1/4 cup diced celery
- 1/4 cup diced bell pepper
- 1 tablespoon lemon juice
- 2 avocados, halved and pitted
- Salt and pepper to taste

Nutritional Values (per serving):

Calories: 250, Protein: 15g, Fat: 18g,
Carbohydrates: 10g, Fiber: 7g, Sugar: 2g

CHICKEN SALAD LETTUCE WRAPS

Prep Time: 10 mins   **Cook Time: 00 mins**   **Serving: 4**

INGREDIENTS

- 2 cups shredded cooked chicken
- 1/4 cup mayonnaise
- 1/4 cup diced celery
- 1 tablespoon Dijon mustard
- 8 large lettuce leaves (Romaine or butter lettuce)
- Salt and pepper to taste

INSTRUCTIONS

1. In a deep-bottom bowl, toss the shredded chicken, mayonnaise, diced celery, and Dijon mustard.
2. Powder it with salt and crushed pepper to taste.
3. Place chicken salad with a spoon into the lettuce leaves. Serve immediately.

Nutritional Values (per serving):

Calories: 200, Protein: 16g, Fat: 12g,
Carbohydrates: 4g, Fiber: 2g, Sugar: 1g

VEGGIE SUSHI ROLLS

Prep Time: 20 mins **Cook Time: 00 mins** **Serving: 4**

INGREDIENTS

- 4 sheets nori
- 2 cups sushi rice, cooked and cooled
- 1/2 cucumber, julienned
- 1/2 carrot, julienned
- 1/2 avocado, sliced
- Soy sauce for serving

INSTRUCTIONS

1. Lay a nori sheet smoothly on a bamboo mat. Spread 1/2 cup of sushi rice evenly over the nori, leaving one-inch border at the top.
2. Arrange the cucumber, carrot, and avocado slices horizontally across the center of the rice.
3. Roll the nori tightly using the sushi mat, wetting the border with water to seal it.
4. Repeat with the leftover nori sheets and fillings. Slice each roll into 6 pieces. Serve with soy sauce.

Nutritional Values (per serving):

Calories: 180, Protein: 4g, Fat: 5g,
Carbohydrates: 30g, Fiber: 4g, Sugar: 2g

INGREDIENTS

- 4 mini bagels, split
- 1/2 cup tomato sauce
- 1 cup shredded mozzarella cheese
- 16 pepperoni slices

MINI BAGEL PIZZAS

Prep Time: 10 mins   **Cook Time: 10 mins**   **Serving: 4**

INSTRUCTIONS

1. Preheat oven to 375°F (190°C). Place the mini bagel halves on the paper-arranged baking sheet.
2. Spread one tbsp tomato sauce on every half of the bagel.
3. Sprinkle with shredded cheese and top with pepperoni slices.
4. Bake for 8-10 minutes until the cheese melts and bubbly. Serve warm.

Nutritional Values (per serving):

Calories: 250, Protein: 12g, Fat: 10g,
Carbohydrates: 28g, Fiber: 2g, Sugar: 4g

INGREDIENTS

- 4 large flour tortillas
- 2 cups cooked chicken, shredded
- 1 cup shredded cheese (cheddar or Monterey Jack)
- 1/2 cup salsa
- 1 tablespoon butter

CHICKEN QUESADILLA WEDGES

Prep Time: 10 mins   **Cook Time: 10 mins**   **Serving: 4**

INSTRUCTIONS

1. Put the non-stick skillet over medium heat to melt the butter.
2. Place a tortilla in the skillet and sprinkle half of the shredded cheese on one half of the tortilla.
3. Add the shredded chicken and salsa on top of the cheese. Sprinkle the leftover cheese over the chicken and salsa.
4. Fold the tortilla in half. Cook for 2-3 minutes on every side until the tortilla is crispy.
5. Repeat with the leftover tortillas. Cut every quesadilla into wedges and serve warm.

Nutritional Values (per serving):

Calories: 350, Protein: 20g, Fat: 15g,
Carbohydrates: 30g, Fiber: 2g, Sugar: 3g

SNACKS

APPLE "COOKIES"

Prep Time: 10 mins   **Cook Time: 00 mins**   **Serving: 4**

INSTRUCTIONS

1. Spread peanut butter (a thin layer) on every apple slice.
2. Sprinkle granola and raisins on top of the peanut butter. Serve immediately.

INGREDIENTS

- 2 apples, cored and sliced horizontally into rounds
- 1/4 cup peanut butter
- 1/4 cup granola
- 2 tablespoons raisins

Nutritional Values (per serving):

Calories: 150, Protein: 3g, Fat: 6g,
Carbohydrates: 23g, Fiber: 4g, Sugar: 16g

CELERY "CATERPILLARS"

Prep Time: 10 mins   **Cook Time: 00 mins**   **Serving: 4**

INGREDIENTS

- 4 celery sticks, cut into 3-inch pieces
- 1/4 cup cream cheese
- 1/4 cup cucumber slices, cut into small rounds
- 2 tablespoons raisins

INSTRUCTIONS

1. Fill each celery stick with cream cheese.
2. Place cucumber slices along the sides of the celery sticks to form legs.
3. Add raisins on top of the cream cheese for eyes. Serve immediately.

Nutritional Values (per serving):

Calories: 60, Protein: 1g, Fat: 4g,
Carbohydrates: 6g, Fiber: 1g, Sugar: 4g

MINI FRUIT KABOBS

Prep Time: 10 mins   **Cook Time: 00 mins**   **Serving: 4**

INGREDIENTS

- 1 cup grapes
- 1 cup strawberries, hulled and halved
- 1 cup pineapple chunks
- 12 toothpicks

INSTRUCTIONS

1. Thread grapes, strawberry halves, and pineapple chunks onto toothpicks.
2. Serve immediately.

Nutritional Values (per serving):

Calories: 50, Protein: 1g, Fat: 0g,
Carbohydrates: 13g, Fiber: 2g, Sugar: 10g

FROZEN YOGURT BITES

Prep Time: 10 mins   **Cook Time: 00 mins**   **Serving: 4**

INGREDIENTS

- 1 cup flavored yogurt
- 1/2 cup mixed fruit (e.g., berries, diced peaches)
- Mini muffin tin

INSTRUCTIONS

1. Spoon the flavored yogurt into the mini muffin tin, filling each cup about three-quarters full.
2. Top with mixed fruit. Freeze until solid, about 2-3 hours.
3. Remove from the mini muffin tin and serve immediately.

Adding ice cream on top to give step this treat up to the next level.

Nutritional Values (per serving):

Calories: 80, Protein: 3g, Fat: 2g,
Carbohydrates: 12g, Fiber: 1g, Sugar: 10g

INGREDIENTS

- 1 zucchini, thinly sliced
- 2 carrots, thinly sliced
- 1 tablespoon olive oil
- 1/2 teaspoon salt
- 1/2 cup ranch dip

VEGGIE "CHIPS" AND DIP

Prep Time: 15 mins   **Cook Time: 20 mins**   **Serving: 4**

INSTRUCTIONS

1. Preheat oven to 400°F (200°C). Toss the zucchini and carrot slices in olive oil and salt.
2. Arrange the veggie slices in one layer on the paper-arranged baking sheet.
3. Bake for 16-20 minutes until crispy, turning halfway through.
4. Serve with Ranch or Salsa dip.

Nutritional Values (per serving):

Calories: 90, Protein: 1g, Fat: 7g,
Carbohydrates: 7g, Fiber: 2g, Sugar: 3g

CHEESE AND CRACKERS

Prep Time: 5 mins   **Cook Time: 00 mins**   **Serving: 4**

INGREDIENTS

- 1 cup assorted cheese slices (cheddar, Swiss, mozzarella)
- 1 cup whole grain crackers

INSTRUCTIONS

1. Let kids assemble their own cheese and cracker combinations.
2. Serve immediately.

Nutritional Values (per serving):

Calories: 200, Protein: 8g, Fat: 12g, Carbohydrates: 16g, Fiber: 2g, Sugar: 2g

POPCORN BALLS

Prep Time: 10 mins   **Cook Time: 5 mins**   **Serving: 4**

INGREDIENTS

- 4 cups popped popcorn
- 1/4 cup honey or maple syrup
- 1/4 cup butter
- 1/2 teaspoon vanilla extract

INSTRUCTIONS

1. In a saucepan, combine honey or maple syrup and butter.
2. Cook over moderate flame until melted and well combined. Then remove and stir in vanilla extract.
3. Ladle mixture over the popped popcorn and mix well to coat.
4. Shape the popcorn into balls and let set on a parchment-lined baking sheet. Serve once set.

Nutritional Values (per serving):

Calories: 150, Protein: 1g, Fat: 8g,
Carbohydrates: 20g, Fiber: 2g, Sugar: 12g

BANANA SUSHI

Prep Time: 5 mins	**Cook Time: 00 mins**	**Serving: 2**

INGREDIENTS

- 1 whole wheat tortilla
- 2 tablespoons peanut butter
- 1 banana

INSTRUCTIONS

1. Spread peanut butter evenly over the whole wheat tortilla.
2. Place the banana on one edge of the tortilla and roll it up tightly. Slice into rounds. Serve immediately.

Nutritional Values (per serving):

Calories: 220, Protein: 6g, Fat: 10g,
Carbohydrates: 30g, Fiber: 4g, Sugar: 12g

INGREDIENTS

- 2 cups seedless grapes

FROZEN GRAPES

Prep Time: 5 mins	Cook Time: 00 mins	Serving: 4

INSTRUCTIONS

1. Wash and dry the grapes. Place the grapes in one layer on the paper-arranged baking sheet.
2. Freeze for two hours or until completely frozen. Serve as a refreshing and sweet treat.

Nutritional Values (per serving):

Calories: 50, Protein: 0g, Fat: 0g,
Carbohydrates: 13g, Fiber: 1g, Sugar: 11g

TRAIL MIX

Prep Time: 5 mins | **Cook Time: 00 mins** | **Serving: 4**

INSTRUCTIONS

1. Take the large shallow bowl and toss the nuts with seeds, dried fruit, and whole grain cereal.
2. Divide into individual portions. Serve immediately or store in an air-sealed jar/container.

INGREDIENTS

- 1 cup mixed nuts (almonds, cashews, peanuts)
- 1/2 cup seeds (pumpkin seeds, sunflower seeds)
- 1/2 cup dried fruit (raisins, cranberries, apricots)
- 1 cup whole grain cereal

Nutritional Values (per serving):

Calories: 200, Protein: 6g, Fat: 12g,
Carbohydrates: 20g, Fiber: 3g, Sugar: 10g

DINNER

BUILD-YOUR-OWN TACOS

Prep Time: 10 mins   **Cook Time: 10 mins**   **Serving: 4**

INGREDIENTS

- 8 taco shells
- 1 pound ground beef or turkey, cooked
- 1 cup shredded cheese
- 1 cup shredded lettuce
- 1 cup salsa

INSTRUCTIONS

1. Set out the taco shells, cooked ground beef or turkey, shredded cheese, lettuce, and salsa.
2. Let kids assemble their own tacos by filling the taco shells with their preferred toppings. Serve immediately.

Nutritional Values (per serving):

Calories: 300, Protein: 18g, Fat: 15g, Carbohydrates: 24g, Fiber: 4g, Sugar: 3g

PIZZA STUFFED BELL PEPPERS

Prep Time: 10 mins   **Cook Time: 20 mins**   **Serving: 4**

INGREDIENTS

- 4 bell peppers, halved and seeded
- 1 cup tomato sauce
- 1 cup shredded mozzarella cheese
- 1 cup favorite pizza toppings (pepperoni, mushrooms, olives, etc.)

INSTRUCTIONS

1. Preheat oven to 375°F (190°C). Place the bell pepper halves on the parchment paper-arranged baking sheet.
2. Fill each half with 2 tablespoons of tomato sauce. Sprinkle shredded cheese on top and spread your favorite pizza toppings.
3. Bake for 20 minutes or until the peppers are tender and the cheese is melted. Serve warm.

Nutritional Values (per serving):

Calories: 200, Protein: 10g, Fat: 10g,
Carbohydrates: 15g, Fiber: 4g, Sugar: 6g

CHICKEN AND VEGGIE STIR-FRY

Prep Time: 15 mins   **Cook Time: 10 mins**   **Serving: 4**

INGREDIENTS

- 2 cups cooked chicken, shredded
- 2 tablespoons olive oil
- 1 cup broccoli florets
- 1 cup sliced bell peppers
- 1 cup chopped carrots
- 1 cup snap peas
- 1/4 cup soy sauce
- 1 tablespoon honey
- 1 teaspoon minced garlic

INSTRUCTIONS

1. Heat two tbsp oil in a skillet over medium-high heat. Add broccoli, bell peppers, and snap peas, chopped carrots, and stir-fry for 5-7 minutes.

2. Add the cooked chicken to the skillet. In a small bowl, toss the soy sauce, honey, and minced garlic.

3. Drop the sauce over the chicken & veggies, and stir-fry for another 5 minutes or until everything is heated through. Serve immediately.

Nutritional Values (per serving):

Calories: 250, Protein: 20g, Fat: 10g,
Carbohydrates: 20g, Fiber: 4g, Sugar: 10g

SPAGHETTI SQUASH "PASTA"

Prep Time: 10 mins   **Cook Time: 40 mins**   **Serving: 4**

INGREDIENTS

- 2 spaghetti squash, halved and seeded
- 2 cups marinara sauce
- 1 cup grated Parmesan cheese
- 2 tablespoons olive oil
- Salt and pepper to taste

INSTRUCTIONS

1. Preheat oven to 400°F (200°C). Drizzle two tbsp oil over the cut sides of the spaghetti squash and powder it with salt and crushed pepper.

2. Place the squash halves cut side down on the parchment paper-arranged baking sheet.

3. Roast for 37-40 minutes until the squash is tender and easily shredded with a fork.

4. Remove and cool slightly. Use a fork to scrape out the spaghetti-like strands into a bowl. Serve with marinara sauce and grated cheese. Serve warm.

Nutritional Values (per serving):

Calories: 180, Protein: 8g, Fat: 10g,
Carbohydrates: 20g, Fiber: 4g, Sugar: 10g

DIY PASTA SALAD

Prep Time: 10 mins   **Cook Time: 10 mins**   **Serving: 4**

INSTRUCTIONS

1. Take the large shallow bowl and combine the cooked pasta, diced vegetables, and cheese cubes.
2. Drop the Italian dressing over the mixture and toss to coat.
3. Let kids mix and serve immediately or chill in the refrigerator until ready to eat.

INGREDIENTS

- 2 cups cooked pasta (any shape)
- 1 cup diced vegetables (bell peppers, cucumbers, cherry tomatoes)
- 1 cup cheese cubes (cheddar, mozzarella)
- 1/2 cup Italian dressing

Nutritional Values (per serving):

Calories: 250, Protein: 10g, Fat: 12g,
Carbohydrates: 26g, Fiber: 2g, Sugar: 4g

BAKED CHICKEN TENDERS

Prep Time: 10 mins **Cook Time: 20 mins** **Serving: 4**

INGREDIENTS

- 1 pound chicken breast, cut into strips
- 1 cup breadcrumbs
- 1/2 cup grated Parmesan cheese
- 1 teaspoon paprika
- 1/2 teaspoon garlic powder
- 1/2 teaspoon salt
- 1/4 teaspoon black pepper
- 1/2 cup milk
- Dipping sauces (ranch, BBQ, honey mustard)

INSTRUCTIONS

1. Preheat oven to 400°F (200°C). In a deep-bottom bowl, combine breadcrumbs, Parmesan cheese, paprika, garlic powder, salt, and black pepper.
2. Dip every meat strip into the milk, then coat with the breadcrumb mixture.
3. Place the coated meat strips on the parchment paper-arranged baking sheet.
4. Bake for 17-20 minutes until the meat is cooked through and crispy. Serve with dipping sauces.

Nutritional Values (per serving):

Calories: 300, Protein: 25g, Fat: 10g,
Carbohydrates: 20g, Fiber: 1g, Sugar: 2g

INGREDIENTS

- 2 cups cooked rice
- 1 cup diced vegetables (carrots, peas, bell peppers)
- 2 eggs, scrambled
- 2 tablespoons soy sauce
- 1 tablespoon olive oil
- 1 teaspoon minced garlic
- 1 teaspoon minced ginger

VEGGIE FRIED RICE

Prep Time: 10 mins   **Cook Time: 10 mins**   **Serving: 4**

INSTRUCTIONS

1. Heat one tbsp oil in a skillet over medium-high heat. Add mashed garlic and ginger, and stir-fry for 1 minute.
2. Add diced vegetables and cook for 3-4 minutes until tender.
3. Add prepared rice and soy sauce and stir to combine. Push the rice to one side of the skillet and add the scrambled eggs, cooking until set.
4. Mix the eggs into the rice and vegetables. Serve immediately.

Nutritional Values (per serving):

Calories: 250, Protein: 8g, Fat: 8g, Carbohydrates: 35g, Fiber: 3g, Sugar: 3g

STUFFED BELL PEPPERS

Prep Time: 10 mins   **Cook Time: 20 mins**   **Serving: 4**

INGREDIENTS

- 4 bell peppers, halved and seeded
- 1 cup cooked quinoa
- 1 cup black beans, drained and rinsed
- 1 cup corn kernels
- 1 cup shredded cheese (cheddar, Monterey Jack)
- 1/2 teaspoon cumin
- 1/2 teaspoon chili powder
- Salt and pepper to taste

INSTRUCTIONS

1. Preheat oven to 375°F (190°C). Take the large shallow bowl and combine the cooked quinoa, black beans, corn, shredded cheese, cumin, chili powder, salt, and crushed pepper.
2. Fill every bell pepper half with the quinoa mixture. Place the stuffed bell peppers on the parchment paper-arranged baking sheet and bake for 17-20 minutes until the peppers are tender. Serve warm.

Nutritional Values (per serving):

Calories: 250, Protein: 12g, Fat: 10g, Carbohydrates: 30g, Fiber: 8g, Sugar: 6g

TURKEY AND VEGGIE MEATBALLS

Prep Time: 15 mins   **Cook Time: 20 mins**   **Serving: 4**

INGREDIENTS

- 1 pound ground turkey
- 1/2 cup grated carrots
- 1/2 cup grated zucchini
- 1/2 cup breadcrumbs
- 1 egg
- 1/4 cup grated Parmesan cheese
- 1 teaspoon garlic powder
- 1 teaspoon onion powder
- 1/2 teaspoon salt
- 1/4 teaspoon black pepper

INSTRUCTIONS

1. Preheat oven to 375°F (190°C). Take the large shallow bowl, toss the ground turkey, grated carrots, grated zucchini, breadcrumbs, egg, Parmesan cheese, garlic, onion powder, salt, and crushed pepper until well combined.
2. Form the mixture into small meatballs and place them on the parchment paper-arranged baking sheet.
3. Bake for 17-20 minutes until the meatballs are done properly and golden brown. Serve warm.

Nutritional Values (per serving):

Calories: 200, Protein: 25g, Fat: 8g,
Carbohydrates: 8g, Fiber: 2g, Sugar: 2g

MINI TURKEY AND CHEESE SLIDERS

Prep Time: 10 mins   **Cook Time: 10 mins**   **Serving: 4**

INGREDIENTS

- 8 slider buns
- 8 slices deli turkey
- 8 slices cheese (cheddar, Swiss, or your choice)
- 1/4 cup mayonnaise
- 1 tablespoon Dijon mustard

INSTRUCTIONS

1. Preheat oven to 350°F (175°C). Slice the slider buns in half and place the bottom halves on a baking sheet.
2. Spread mayonnaise and Dijon mustard on every bun. Layer a slice of deli turkey and a slice of cheese on every bun.
3. Place the top halves of the buns on the sliders.
4. Bake for 8-10 minutes until cheese melts completely and the buns are toasted. Serve warm.

Nutritional Values (per serving):

Calories: 250, Protein: 15g, Fat: 12g,
Carbohydrates: 20g, Fiber: 2g, Sugar: 3g

DESSERTS

FRUIT SALAD

Prep Time: 10 mins **Cook Time: 00 mins** **Serving: 4**

INGREDIENTS

- 1 cup strawberries, hulled and sliced
- 1 cup grapes, halved
- 1 cup melon, cubed
- 1 apple, diced
- 1 tablespoon lemon juice

INSTRUCTIONS

1. Take the large shallow bowl and combine the strawberries, grapes, melon, and apple.
2. Drizzle lemon juice and toss properly to coat. Serve immediately.

Nutritional Values (per serving):

Calories: 60, Protein: 1g, Fat: 0g,
Carbohydrates: 15g, Fiber: 3g, Sugar: 12g

FROZEN BANANA POPS

Prep Time: 10 mins **Cook Time: 00 mins** **Serving: 4**

INGREDIENTS

- 4 bananas, peeled and halved
- 8 popsicle sticks
- 1 cup yogurt or melted chocolate
- 1/2 cup sprinkles or chopped nuts (optional)

INSTRUCTIONS

1. Insert a popsicle stick into every half banana. Dip the bananas into yogurt or melted chocolate, coating them evenly.
2. Roll in sprinkles or chopped nuts if desired. Place the banana pops on a parchment-arranged baking sheet and freeze for two hours. Serve frozen.

Nutritional Values (per serving):

Calories: 150, Protein: 3g, Fat: 4g,
Carbohydrates: 30g, Fiber: 3g, Sugar: 18g

INGREDIENTS

- 3 tablespoons butter
- 4 cups mini marshmallows
- 6 cups Rice Krispies cereal

RICE KRISPIE TREATS

Prep Time: 10 mins   **Cook Time: 5 mins**   **Serving: 16 squares**

INSTRUCTIONS

1. In a pot, melt the butter. Add the mini marshmallows and toss well until completely melted and smooth.
2. Remove and add Rice Krispies cereal, stirring until well coated.
3. Press the mixture toward the bottom of a greased 9x13-inch pan using a buttered spatula or wax paper.
4. Let cool completely before cutting into squares. Serve.

Nutritional Values (per serving):

Calories: 90, Protein: 1g, Fat: 2g,
Carbohydrates: 18g, Fiber: 0g, Sugar: 8g

CHOCOLATE-DIPPED STRAWBERRIES

 Prep Time: 10 mins   **Cook Time: 00 mins**   **Serving: 4**

INGREDIENTS

- 1 cup chocolate chips (milk, dark, or white)
- 1 tablespoon coconut oil (optional)
- 1 pint of strawberries, washed and dried

INSTRUCTIONS

1. In a heavy glass bowl, melt the chocolate chips and coconut oil (if using) in 30-second intervals (in a microwave), stirring after each, until smooth.
2. Dip every dried strawberry into the melted chocolate, allowing any excess to drip off.
3. Place the dipped strawberries on a parchment-arranged baking sheet.
4. Refrigerate until the chocolate is set, about 15-20 minutes. Serve chilled.

Nutritional Values (per serving):

Calories: 120, Protein: 1g, Fat: 7g, Carbohydrates: 15g, Fiber: 2g, Sugar: 12g

INGREDIENTS

- 2 cups flavored yogurt
- 1/2 cup mixed berries
- 1/4 cup granola

FROZEN YOGURT BARK

Prep Time: 10 mins **Cook Time: 00 mins** **Serving: 4**

INSTRUCTIONS

1. Spread the flavored yogurt evenly onto a parchment-arranged baking sheet.
2. Sprinkle the mixed berries and granola over the yogurt. Freeze for at least 2 hours or until firm.
3. Break into pieces and serve frozen.

Nutritional Values (per serving):

Calories: 100, Protein: 4g, Fat: 2g,
Carbohydrates: 18g, Fiber: 2g, Sugar: 12g

INGREDIENTS

- 4 ripe bananas, sliced and frozen

BANANA "ICE CREAM"

Prep Time: 5 mins   **Cook Time: 00 mins**   **Serving: 4**

INSTRUCTIONS

1. Add frozen banana slices into the food blender. Blend until the texture turns smooth and creamy, scraping down the sides as needed.
2. Serve immediately as soft-serve or freeze for an additional 30 minutes for a firmer texture.

Nutritional Values (per serving):

Calories: 90, Protein: 1g, Fat: 0g,
Carbohydrates: 23g, Fiber: 3g, Sugar: 12g

HOMEMADE FRUIT POPSICLES

Prep Time: 10 mins   **Cook Time: 00 mins**   **Serving: 4**

INGREDIENTS

- 2 cups fruit juice (any flavor)
- 1 cup pureed fruit (berries, mango, peach)

INSTRUCTIONS

1. In a deep-bottom bowl, mix the fruit juice and pureed fruit. Pour the mixture into popsicle molds.
2. Freeze for four hours or until solid. Serve frozen.

Nutritional Values (per serving):

Calories: 70, Protein: 0g, Fat: 0g,
Carbohydrates: 18g, Fiber: 1g, Sugar: 14g

INGREDIENTS

- 4 apples, peeled and sliced
- 1 teaspoon cinnamon
- 1/4 cup rolled oats
- 1/4 cup brown sugar
- 2 tablespoons butter, melted

APPLE CRISP

Prep Time: 15 mins   **Cook Time: 30 mins**   **Serving: 4**

INSTRUCTIONS

1. Preheat oven to 350°F (175°C). In a deep-bottom bowl, mix the apple slices with cinnamon.
2. Spread the apple slices evenly (make sure they don't overlap) in a baking dish.
3. In another bowl, combine the rolled oats, brown sugar, and melted butter.
4. Sprinkle the oat mixture over the apples. Bake for 27-30 minutes until the apples are tende. Serve warm.

Nutritional Values (per serving):

Calories: 150, Protein: 1g, Fat: 4g, Carbohydrates: 30g, Fiber: 4g, Sugar: 20g

INGREDIENTS

- 2 cups flavored yogurt
- 1/2 cup granola
- 1/2 cup mixed berries

YOGURT PARFAIT POPSICLES

Prep Time: 10 mins   **Cook Time: 00 mins**   **Serving: 4**

INSTRUCTIONS

1. Layer the flavored yogurt, granola, and mixed berries in popsicle molds, alternating between each layer.
2. Freeze for at least 4 hours or until solid. Serve frozen.

Nutritional Values (per serving):

Calories: 120, Protein: 5g, Fat: 3g, Carbohydrates: 20g, Fiber: 2g, Sugar: 12g

INGREDIENTS

- 1 cup rolled oats
- 1/2 cup peanut butter
- 1/4 cup honey
- 1/4 cup chocolate chips

NO-BAKE ENERGY BITES

Prep Time: 10 mins   **Cook Time: 00 mins**   **Serving: 12 bites**

INSTRUCTIONS

1. Take the large shallow bowl and toss the rolled oats, peanut butter, honey, and chocolate chips until well combined.
2. Roll the mixture into bite-sized balls. Place on the parchment paper-arranged baking sheet and refrigerate for 30 minutes or until firm. Serve chilled.

Nutritional Values (per serving):

Calories: 100, Protein: 3g, Fat: 5g,
Carbohydrates: 12g, Fiber: 2g, Sugar: 7g

Conclusion

Congratulations on completing your culinary journey with Yummy Adventures: Cooking with Kids! We hope this cookbook has provided you and your young chefs with countless hours of fun and deliciousness in the kitchen. By now, you've discovered that cooking together is not only a great way to create tasty meals but also a fantastic opportunity to bond, learn, and make lasting memories.

As you continue to explore new recipes and refine your skills, remember that the most important ingredient in any dish is love. Encourage your kids to experiment, be creative, and most importantly, enjoy the process. Whether you're whipping up a quick snack or preparing a full meal, the time spent together in the kitchen is truly invaluable.

Thank you for joining us on this yummy adventure. We hope these recipes become family favorites and inspire a lifelong love of cooking in your children. Keep cooking, keep experimenting, and keep making delicious memories together. Happy cooking!

Thank you so much for reading this book and we hope you've enjoyed it, please consider some of the cookbooks in the following series

Book Series - Around the World in Tasty Ways:
https://geni.us/AroundTastyWaysSeries
Featuring cuisines from Spain, Italy, France, California, China and many more!

This collection of cookbooks brings the vibrant flavors of global cuisines right to your kitchen. From spicy Indian curries to savory Italian pastas, each book in this series explores a different corner of the world, offering authentic recipes and cultural insights. Whether you're craving the bold flavors of Paris or the delicate tastes of California, this collection has something for every palate. Join us on a journey of culinary discovery and explore the diverse and delicious cuisines of the world.

Book Series - Culinary Chronicles, Cooking with Passion:
https://geni.us/CulinaryChroniclesDL
Featuring Cuisines using Air Fryers, Grills, preparing appetizers, Dairy and Gluten free books too.
Introducing our diverse collection of cookbooks that revolutionize the way you approach meal preparation. Instead of focusing on specific countries, our collection delves into different styles of cooking and meal areas, ensuring a comprehensive exploration of culinary delights.

With our collection of cookbooks, you'll embark on a culinary adventure that transcends borders, bringing the world's flavors right to your kitchen. Whether you're entertaining guests or enjoying a cozy night in, these cookbooks are sure to inspire and delight.

View the full range of our publishing at our website
https://soreadytoread.com

For Cookbooks, Coloring, Technology and Self-development books or sport, there is something for everyone, of all ages, at SoReadyToRead.com

Sign up to our distribution list to be the first to discover new titles and promotions.

Made in the USA
Coppell, TX
04 December 2024

41751977R10066